A Lost Kite

For the few who live with a heart
full of love,
are the same to discover
treasures deep within.

Inspired are those with beautiful
spirits.

Walk with love, and you'll talk
with love,
Give your love and you'll receive
love.

So... dwell in an ocean filled with
people in harmony.

Admire the stars that mimic
your creation.

What you see in a mirror is who

I AM

BY
ANDRE PRICE

ISBN-10:1732077606
ISBN-13: 978-1732077607

you are.

A reflection of what was, and the
potential
of what might always be.

My wish is distant from its
belief,
A belief even further from my
faith.

It fades into my will, to look
inside...
Instead I look away.

Why so complicated?
Over and over I make the same
mistakes.

Unanswered questions until a
sudden...bang...
A realization in a moment.

Two extremes collide... suddenly
a gut feeling,
Something has transpired.

Something, unexplainable on
the surface;
But deep down, instantly
understood.

I've been Happy and I 've been
stressed...
Been through hell, been in
love...
Been through up and downs.
Underestimated...
But now, I’m free!

Free to live and free to love.

Free yourself from your past.
Unleash the power we all

possess.

I’m sorry... Life's full of mistakes
and
second chances, no excuse can
mend
my lack of compassion.

I’ve ignored my heart and let my
ego
lead for too long, jeopardizing
family
and friends.

Time tells all... it's time to step
to the plate.
Looking out and not within;
makes one lose focus.

Blinded from living the truth.
Without truth is not knowing
thyself.

How can I love... without loving
myself?

Your love I've known more
personally than most,
never loved by words or
anything, but a loving nature.

The obvious force of power
never hides... I’m sorry.

The Beginnings
(Man N' the Mirror)

Plenty of times things seem so
all of a sudden,
Some call it luck, better yet...
coincidence.

Reality is... everything happens
for a reason.
We may not understand the
reason...
But it happens.

For instance, if you're a football
player
and you catch a pass with one
hand,
most people will call it luck.

Other way to see it is: he put the

time in,
the effort to accomplish
whatever needs be.

People forget; we only do things
the way
we were taught, or the way we've
seen things done.

Could've been the wrong way
the whole time,
but this is all that you know...
until otherwise.

Start thinking for yourself and
doing things
your way, you will see what you
supposed to see...

Sort of like religion. Base your
beliefs on what
everyone around you believes,

read the Bible, Quran, etc.

Sometimes you don't understand what you are reading. You have to do it your way. Your way might not be my way or his way, but it's your way. That's all that matters.

Establish a relationship with "The All", "God" or a "Higher Power". It may seem wrong to those around you, however, at the end of the day, Its between you and The Man Above.

It has to come from within. Know what its not and what it is. Who can

judge? When you
start understanding life and the
human
responses; it's life at it's highest.

When the universe speaks… we
listen.
Everything else stops, know how
to communicate.
Be one with your higher self,
everything else stops.
You have to know how to
communicate
and stay one with your higher
self.

Everything around us can be a
message at any
point in time. Know your
moves, know your
purpose and know your route.
Make progress

and everything else is irrelevant.
Those who fall off, served their
purpose.

It may be hard to dismiss the
emotions that come
with it, but you have to stay in
control.
They can alter your decisions
moving forward.
Life happens... whether you
agree with every moment,
accept it and keep it moving.
Don't dwell on it too long.

What you see, is what was
meant for you to see.
What was done, was meant to be
done. Finding
truth is finding life, once you
found life...
you found a reason to live.

Moments define time, what do
you spend your time on?
Nothing is set in stone and can
change at any moment,
do you keep an open mind?

They say it's either black or
white, what they don't say
is there's always a grey area.

It's meeting in the middle,
understanding,
two parties being neutral.

White can't transform into black
without grey involved
and vise versa; Understanding
there is always a bigger
picture, should motivate you to
keep reaching.

Honesty to self is an important
task.
Every day can be used as a
stepping stone.
If I speak or act in a certain way;
I pay attention to thyself,
analyzing the situation from a
clear perspective.
Ignoring my own flaws hurts me
in the long run.
I stay aware consistently...
Embrace yourself or change
yourself,
I choose to embrace and change
myself.

Being persistent helps me see
growth.
It's satisfying to know you can
do what's needed.
Know yourself and your time
worth.

Every one is different.
That's why you have to know
yourself,
before you can understand
someone else.

When you look in the mirror;
what do you see?
I see someone who is trying to
show others,
that our life is what we make of
it.
No matter the situation we are
in control of our own...
We are our own enemy, that's
truth.

It's said that the truth hurts... do
you know the truth?
The truth is us, it's you, it's me.

Understanding there is a time to

grow up, and become
our own. We have to question
everything we think we know.
When we question ourselves we
make our own decisions;
we can either lie, or be satisfied
with what we already know.
Being honest knowing that we
know nothing.

Ideas are shaped from the
environment around us,
blind are many people to this
fact.

Beliefs and opinions not being
their own.
Truth isn't their truth... it's his,
it's hers.

Question yourself, don't be
afraid to face the man in the

mirror.
You have to loose yourself, to
find yourself.

Life is a constant battle, so don't
be afraid of the challenge.
There is always more, so don't
settle for less.

Getting comfortable with self
freezes a creative spark and
stunts growth.
Giving time a bad name, making
space for an ego.
A river of thoughts flow without
them,
with a storm every now and
again.

Embracing natural battles and
becoming stronger.
Discomfort is good for growth, it

strengthens you
in ways far and beyond. The
universe plays one song,
those who find truth,
understand being one with all.

Thoughts manifest themselves
observing actions,
inevitably increasing self
awareness as we evolve.
Accept fear as the illusion it is.
We ultimately knock
down all walls. On the road to
finding one's self
you'll find the one presence all
humanity searches for.

My Passion (Dancing with Destiny)

Tonight my confidence decided
to dance,
with all of me and anything
extra I drag with me .

My mind, body and soul drowns
in infinite love,

By staying in harmony and
constantly reflecting.
Hidden treasures burned in my
conscience.

Understanding human nature, is
seeing heaven bless the blessed.

Stop resisting and become one
with her.
Drowning ultimately becomes
reality,
In it's trust is now, then and
forever.
Sleeping is for those who are not
awake.
Eternity is internal, listen to the
rhythm of the music.

Put energy into synchronizing
with it.
The differences that embrace,
shine light on individuality.
The transformation made after
years of broken hearts;
broken promises, and fake love.

The law delivered truth with
time and hard work,
Accepted loosing is for those

who accept it and
get attached. I learned my
lesson by respecting
the task and seeing it for what it
truly is.
My past love is a foundation I've
build upon.

It's the force of life... life having
faith in the universe.

In myself daily, my love to
become a better vessel.

Balanced evolution and self
awareness are the keys to
growth.
Accepting myself and my truth, I
accept death for what it is,
Natural... nothing more.

Seeing fear as the illusion it is.

I take pleasure in fighting the
silent war.

Dancing with destiny motivates
me more and more.
Being accepted in the "
university of true religion"
built an infinite supply of
happiness.
Respecting the struggles and
hardships that I unfortunately
held captive.

Alone can only be the blame
being blinded,
by anything means being
blinded to self.
The art of suggestion keeps my
mind on the hunt for hidden
forces.
Attacking my mind, body and
soul.

Episodes encountered tend to
have dramatic effects
on my heart. While adapting we
become more familiar
to the sudden shocks.

I recognize when these fears are
at work.

Meditating, staying detached
keeps my mind at peace.
The process of accepting is
shocking!

Normally, I learn how to work
with and not against it.

Having complete faith in
yourself to overcome,
gives power to concur the
situation at hand.

Staying fearless in my pursuit
gives me strength,
to fight through the unknown.
I know I will never see life the
same as I found truth.
It's deeper and much bigger
than human intellect.

Scattered Thoughts (letter to my thoughts)

Lately I've been paying attention
to my reoccurring
thoughts , seems like my most
dominant thought is change.

Changing is a part of humanity,
it's a natural thing...
At times I'm afraid. It's hard to
pinpoint
what I'm afraid of exactly,
I will say that it's the fear of the
unknown.

On the other hand I want
change, and whatever

obstacles come with it. I need to
embrace change
and turn it into a positive.
It's hard to let go of the past.

Why is it so hard to let go? I ask
myself all the time
and the answer continues to
change.

As of right now,
I would say letting go is
not an easy decision.

It is a decision that I struggle
with daily.
I asked my friend why it's so
hard to let go?

He said "you might not be
prepared for what
comes next, or it might not be

time to let go."

In a constant battle within
myself, having to
conquer anything and
everything.
Why do actions speak louder
than words?

While conversing on the phone,
my friend said,
"Seems like we are in a
relationship,
by the way we act towards each
other."

Now mind you; we are only
friends.
As the day went on, my mind
kept replaying our
communication...
human thoughts arose.

I came to a conclusion; words can do harm
as well as good... actions are more powerful.

Instead of preaching, I need to start putting
actions behind my words. I'm a talkative person
who speaks about better days, now it’s time to

live that way. At times I would say one thing
and do another... that’s a contradiction.
I didn’t want to live a lie, while speaking truth.

I’m at a point in my life, where I am coming

into my own. Everything counts,
everything
is for a reason.

I'm building my castle. I'm
building my future.
I have to make sure it's build on
a solid foundation.

The foundation is very vital, I'm
still figuring it out.
I'm starting to understand
myself, at the same time,
I don't understand anything.

The more I grow confident, the
more I feel lost.
Sometimes it feels like no sense
of direction.

I contemplate whether I'm
changing,

for the worst, rather than
changing for the better.
I beat myself up. Sometimes
inside me says,
" I can do better," at the same
time, something
tells me "I m doing what I'm
supposed to.

It's painful. This battle keeps me
on edge.
I'm fighting and giving all that I
have.

I live for my family and that's
my choice.
I make the future what it needs
to be.

I want the responsibility and
everything
that comes with it. I'm am the

man for the job.
Everything I've been through,
has happened for a reason.
I was blind, but now I see.
I will literally die a few
times spiritually, mentally and
see the
beauty in my tragedies.

At the moment I don’t
understand,
why I had to be the one feeling
the wrath.

But it’s all starting to make
sense.
It builds character and kills
pride.

The main reason I went through

all that I
went through, was for me to find
the
presence I have always ignored.

God, The almighty~
I found my reason for living
and gladly accept my role.
I never pictured this, but now
I'm a
man on a mission.

It's going to be a long road
ahead.
I pray for forgiveness for any
wrongs prior,
and for those I commit in the
future.
I'm going full force.

www.ingramcontent.com/pod-product-compliance
Lightning Source LLC
Chambersburg PA
CBHW051818050726
47598CB00006B/2608

* 9 7 8 1 7 3 2 0 7 7 6 0 7 *